You Are the Opportunity You Were Waiting For

The PHILOSOPHY of SUCCESS

in

21

TIMELESS PRINCIPLES

You Are the Opportunity You Were Waiting For

The **PHILOSOPHY** *of* **SUCCESS**

in

21

TIMELESS PRINCIPLES

by

LUIS E. ROMERO

Abstract image with yellow triangles on cover used under license
from Shutterstock.com.

First Edition: October 2014.
Minor edits and cover redesign: August 2016.
Minor edits: June 2020.

Published by
Luis Romero International LLC, Miami, Florida.
Visit the author's website at www.LERomero.com.

ISBN: 978-0-9908959-0-9 (Hardback)
ISBN: 978-0-9886926-7-1 (Paperback)
ISBN: 978-0-9908959-8-5 (eBook)

Printed in the United States of America

This book is dedicated to those who are striving to become the best they can be. To those who are hungry for success and pursue it joyfully and ethically. To those who are willing to improve their ways in order to improve the world. To those who have shown me all of the foregoing in so many different ways.

CONTENTS

Introduction   1

1. You Are the Opportunity You Were   3
    Waiting For

2. Success Is More than Just a List of   5
    Victories

3. Humility Is the Highest of Virtues   7

4. Perfection Is Inevitable; Learning from It Is   9
    a Choice

5. Prudence Is the Offspring of Courage   11

6. Weaknesses Are Blessings in Disguise   13

7. Uniqueness Is an Inner Conquest   15

8. Knowledge Is the Link between Creativity   17
    & Innovation.

9. Knowledge Is Just an Approximation to   19
    Reality

10. Joy Is Different from Pleasure   21

11. Balance Is Meant to Be Temporary   23

CONTENTS (Cont.)

12. Conflict Resolution Is a Necessity   25

13. A Vision for the Future Must Contain a Worldview   27

14. People Are the Mirrors of Truth   29

15. Hope Can Become the Best Cover-up for Fear   31

16. Perseverance Is the Key to Patience   33

17. Self-knowledge Must Be Actionable   35

18. Empathy Is About Self-confidence   37

19. Guilt Alone Engenders No Virtue   39

20. Democracy Is a Daily Conquest   41

21. Nations Rely on Principles to Endure   43

References   45

Introduction

This book is meant to be a simple and powerful manual for everyone pursuing success. The 21 principles presented herein are straightforward yet insightful guidelines that will help you realize your vision.

The Proposition

Whether you make a living as a business owner, a business executive, an entrepreneur, or a freelancer, you are most likely very busy strategizing, organizing, marketing, and selling your products and services. It may be the case that you are indeed so busy with work and life in general, that you lack the time to reassess, reframe, and learn from your own experiences. Furthermore, you may be in search of a simple yet meaningful frame of reference that will help you unpack, digest, and organize the lessons hidden in your daily life.

With the preceding in mind, this text was written to serve you as that frame of reference that you have been seeking. From such intimate matters as self-knowledge and personal growth to imperative social considerations such as democracy and the free-market economy, this manuscript presents 21 timeless principles that make success an achievable aspiration for everyone. These principles are presented straightforwardly so that you can make immediate applications to your life. Also, they were conceived with depth and insight so as to provide you with wisdom and inspiration.

The Source

The principles presented herein resulted from studying the lives of many iconic figures who have been successful on a grand scale in business, politics, and science. I examined their virtues and iniquities as the main factors informing their decisions. Equally important, I analyzed their achievements and failures as key aspects of their legacies. The conclusions were life-changing and run throughout the 21 principles.

Among the icons surveyed were Henry Ford, for his determination and innovative spirit; Walt Disney, for his perseverance and imagination; and Steve Jobs, for his visionary and groundbreaking thinking. Also, Martin Luther King, Jr., Mother Teresa, and Nelson Mandela, for their humility, courage, and self-sacrifice. Last but not least, Leonardo da Vinci, for his curiosity and genius; Charles Darwin, for his inquisitive observation of the natural world; and Albert Einstein, for his revolutionary approach to physics. The lives of these and many other successful figures in history helped shape the 21 timeless principles of success.

The Delivery

In order to make this manuscript as impactful as possible, the icons studied for this project are not individually linked to any of the 21 principles in an explicit way. Yet their aggregate teachings run throughout the whole book. The individual cross-reference would be an academic exercise that would detract from the clarity and power of each principle. Having disclosed this editorial decision, let us get started.

1

You Are the Opportunity You Were Waiting For

Originally, the word opportunity referred to what is inside an individual rather than outside.

The definition we have today for the word "opportunity" is considerably different from its etymological origin. It lacks the existential depth and transformational power of its original version.

Today we use the word "opportunity" to refer to external circumstances that may be favorable to us. According to the Merriam-Webster Dictionary, "opportunity" has the following two meanings: "1) a favorable juncture of circumstances; 2) a good chance for advancement or progress." These definitions determine today's use of this term in colloquial, literary, and business communications.

However, the original connotation of this word referred to the relationship between an individual and his or her external circumstances; and how that individual was able to use them to realize his or her vision. The word "opportunity" comes from the Latin term *opportunitas*,[1] which is the result of combining *ob*, meaning "toward," and *portus*, meaning "port." This term came about in the realm of navigation, where sailors used the phrase *ob portus* to denote the best combination of wind, current, and tide to sail to port. However, the only way to seize such weather conditions was if the vessel's captain had already sighted the port of destination. Knowing the meteorological variables without knowing the destination was useless. Therefore, a ship was in a state of opportunitas when its captain had already decided where to go and knew how to get there. Later, however, the word evolved, or devolved, in a different direction, to denote only external conditions while excluding the individual who would seize them.

If we rescue the original meaning of the word "opportunity," we will realize that we are its best definition. We become our best opportunity by deciding who we want to be and what we want to achieve.[2] This is the philosophy that permeates every chapter of this book. This is how we can assume full responsibility for our actions and start building the future that we really want.

2

Success Is More than Just a List of Victories

Success is a way of learning from both victory and defeat so that advancement becomes inevitable.

Success is a natural human aspiration—even more so in today's competitive society. To this end, we strive for victory and avoid defeat. Yet, sooner or later, everyone learns that defeat is inevitable. Therefore, every success story must account for some mistakes, errors, and undesired results along the way.

The question is, then, how do we account for defeat in the pursuit of success? Well, we do so by learning from it. Success depends upon our ability to learn from both victory and defeat so that advancement becomes inevitable.

In fact, experiencing defeat early in life can be considered a privilege. Those who do not might grow to believe falsely that they are infallible. Years later, when they inevitably fail for the first time, they will have a hard time handling it. Many, in this position, resort to deceit, treachery, and a whole array of misconducts in order to continue to look unbeaten. In so doing, they will rupture teams and damage relationships in ways that will make them fail beyond their worst fears.

Nonetheless, if we see defeat as an opportunity for improvement, then it becomes as valuable as victory, since both can assist us in our continual development. Victory teaches us the best ways to pursue success, while defeat shows us the wrong ways to do so. We need both types of lessons to continue advancing in the pursuit of our vision.

Finally, as we chase after our dreams, we must learn to enjoy our triumphs without resting on our laurels, and to accept our downfalls without letting them demoralize us. Success is the art and science of moving forward regardless of the circumstances, whether positive or negative. It is the ability to remain focused regardless of how happy or sad we feel. Success is a sign of our character.

3

Humility Is the Highest of Virtues

Humility is the antidote to conceit and shame.

If we experience victory with conceit, then we are just as likely to experience defeat with shame. This is because, in both cases, we are experiencing life mainly through our egos, which means that our fear of the opinion of others is the main force driving our actions.

Conceit makes us afraid of others not seeing us in our victory, while shame makes us afraid of others seeing us in our defeat. In both cases, our egos have taken a hold of our inner selves and we feel restless. As a result, we will likely undermine the pursuit of our own vision by devoting part of our energy to trying to mold the way we believe others are seeing us.

If we want to break free from conceit and shame, we must walk the path of humility, devoid of our egos as much as possible. Thus, fear of the opinion of others will no longer be our chief motivator. Neither victory nor defeat will make us afraid of what others may or may not think about us. Both victory and defeat will be equally valuable to us in becoming the person we want to be. They both will teach us what we need to know about ourselves and the people around us, so we can continue to pursue our dreams and be successful. This is why humility is the highest of virtues.[3]

4

Perfection Is Inevitable; Learning from It Is a Choice

Perfection is a wave that can be surfed, not a way to surf the wave.

Perfection is what happens by the laws of nature, specifically, per the law of cause and effect. Therefore, everything that happens anywhere in the universe is perfect by design. In this regard, both our victories and our defeats are perfect because they could not have happened any other way given the way we acted. Only humility allows us to fathom this notion of perfection, which is what makes learning possible.

However, the most common notion of perfection is very different from the foregoing. People tend to believe that perfection is the unfolding of reality according to their wishes. This is a catastrophic view because it is not true—reality is the result of our actions, not our wishes. Therefore, people tend to experience frustration, sadness, and stubbornness when, actually, they should undergo acceptance, reassessment, and learning.

If we want to change our reality, it would be unwise to try to alter the law of cause and effect for it is impossible. Said law is immutable and, for this reason, it is the only reference for true learning. If we want to modify our reality, rather than trying to change the law of cause and effect, we must learn how to cause the effects that we desire. This requires humility, patience, and determination. This is the path to success.

Of course, the law of cause and effect manifests differently depending on what aspect of reality we are observing. If we drop a coin, it will fall to the ground (gravity); similarly, if we restrict the offer of a given product while keeping its demand constant, its price will rise (supply and demand). Still, be it in physics, economics, or any other realm of life, the law of cause and effect will always apply. This is perfection. Therefore, perfection is inevitable; learning from it is a choice.

5

Prudence is the Offspring of Courage

Fear is inevitable, anger is a necessity, courage is a choice, and prudence is mastery.

So-called courage without prior fear is just mindless daring; sheer idiocy. True courage is the result of experiencing and overcoming fear in a way that strengthens our inner selves, so increasing our determination to act, and improving our understanding of the challenges we face. Courage is the child of fear. Yet the path from the latter to the former is an arduous one.

The most primal tool to fight fear is anger. However, anger's only legitimate goal is self-preservation by disabling the enemy. For this reason, if unchanged, anger will grow to become an unharnessed force of destruction. That is why we must use our judgment to transform it into a sustainable creative force. This is how we give rise to courage, that is, the capacity to face our fears, protect our dignity, stand up for our rights, and build the life we want without destroying everything else on our path.

When fear prevails, it is followed by panic and then terror, so leaving us paralyzed or acting with despair. When anger prevails, it is followed by resentment and then hatred, thus turning us into vengeful destroyers of other people; ergo, of ourselves. However, when courage prevails, it becomes the foundation of a life based on true self-respect; ergo, respect for others. Most importantly, when courage prevails, the initial fear that triggered the process is transformed into prudence, one of our most useful virtues.[4]

6

Weaknesses Are Blessings in Disguise

Weaknesses are the seeds of the greatest strengths. Uncontrolled strengths, however, always become weaknesses.

We all have a particular combination of strengths and weaknesses, which makes us highly competent at some tasks and less so at others. This combination, regardless of how balanced or unbalanced, reveals an undeniable truth: no one is infallible. Even when we use our finest strengths, our weaknesses continue to be present, thus influencing our actions in unknown ways. This introduces a level of unpredictability in our lives that can only be mitigated with the disciplined practice of self-knowledge and personal growth.

Although human weaknesses may seem undesirable at first sight, they are indeed a blessing. Whereas our strengths are readily available to help us achieve our goals, our weaknesses require that we develop humility to accept them and courage to overcome them. Interestingly, humility and courage are the greatest human strengths. We need our weaknesses to explore and reach the full extent of our human greatness.

Nevertheless, many people run away from their weaknesses and try to delude themselves into believing they are infallible. This is usually the route of those who have been deeply hurt in the past. That is, those whose weaknesses have been abused by others. People with a history of abuse will dream of being almighty and self-sufficient so that they can defend themselves from future harm. Some, in an attempt to make their dream come true, will overexert their strengths so as to create an illusion of infallibility. Temporarily, this may serve them as an effective mirage. However, as time goes on, their weaknesses, still unaddressed, will pile up, deteriorate, and start eating away at their strengths. This will gradually render these individuals not only highly fallible but actually obsolete.

Consequently, in order to walk the path of success, we must embrace both our strengths and weaknesses. In fact, in the long term, the latter will prove more useful than the former as humility and courage, the ultimate human strengths, flourish only in the soil of weakness.

7

Uniqueness Is an Inner Conquest

Uniqueness is the result of being oneself, not of trying to be different.

In today's highly diverse society, we are told to find what makes us different in order to stand out, make a statement, and be successful. "Do not be like anyone else," we often hear from inspirational speakers and celebrities. The truth is that success is not the result of being different per se; it is the result of knowing and mastering who we are.

In order to find what makes us unique, we had better look inside ourselves and find what makes us tick. Let us not look outside and cling to what makes others talk about us. When we look inside, we are pursuing self-realization, happiness, and transcendence, the only real forms of being unique. But, when we look outside, all we are doing is attracting attention to ourselves, which will inevitably enslave us to public perception and destroy our uniqueness.

Those who become slaves to public perception will, sooner or later, resort to exaggeration and eccentricity to continue to capture the attention of the public. Interestingly, the media portrays said approach as one of the most effective paths to success. Nonetheless, we must look at the other side of the coin. While exaggeration and eccentricity will always have an audience, such forms of self-expression do not coexist well with happiness and self-realization. In fact, they coexist better with anxiety, depression, insecurity, and a restless soul. Furthermore, they often lead to tragedy.

If we choose to walk the path of exaggeration and eccentricity as part of our lives, let us remember the following. Initially, people will pay attention to us. Later, they will get used to us. Finally, they will be bored with us. When this happens, we must decide how much farther we are willing to go in order to keep them interested. The best choice will be to stop sensationalizing ourselves before we hurt ourselves.

However, when people enjoy the thrill of public attention after going out on every limb to get it, they find it very difficult to live without it. This, in turn, usually leads them down a dangerous path of overexposure, self-ridicule, and often, self-harm. In this regard, it is crucial for us to discover, and feel appreciation for, who we really are regardless of the opinions of others. This way, we can remain grounded when we experience positive attention, negative attention, or indifference from other people. That is true uniqueness.

8

Knowledge Is the Link Between Creativity and Innovation

We need knowledge to harness and steer our creative power so we can use it to our benefit.

Creativity takes place in the mind and is fueled by the heart. It is an intellectual process that requires emotional fuel. Once we become inspired, creativity gives us access to the realm of new possibilities, which contains the seeds of change, progress, and evolution.

Creativity has no structure, though. The very nature of the creative process is untamed by the laws of reality. Therefore, unless coupled with something else, it will always end up producing nothing, or even worse, chaos. Creativity needs harnessing and steering in order to transform new possibilities into new realities. Such a complement is provided by knowledge.

Knowledge does have a structure that provides an approximation to the real world. Because of this, knowledge helps us fill in the gaps in our new ideas and get rid of their inconsistencies. In so doing, our ideas can become new products, services, or what have you. That is how knowledge helps creativity turn into innovation, and later, into success.

9

Knowledge Is Just an Approximation to Reality

Whoever wants to be successful must possess knowledge, but most importantly, must be able to challenge it.

Knowledge is used to solve problems, fuel innovation, and promote progress. Therefore, it is instrumental to success. However, it can also be misused to argue in favor of the unjustifiable, abuse others, and produce an illusion of certainty to hide our inability to manage uncertainty. In such cases, knowledge becomes useless—sometimes even counter-productive. It becomes, in fact, just a vehicle to express our conceit, anger, and fear.

No wonder the first biblical metaphor describing human misfortune tells the story of how Adam and Eve lost Paradise when they took the fruit from the tree of knowledge. Of course, there is absolutely nothing wrong with knowledge. The problem is what happens to people when they cling to it as if it were an absolute truth. Knowledge is an approximation to reality, not reality itself. It is relative, not absolute. What was considered knowledge yesterday is considered ignorance today. That is the way it has always been. Therefore, when we cling to current knowledge as if it were an absolute truth, it becomes the seed of ignorance and failure for tomorrow. In this regard, knowledge, as shown throughout human history, is a double-edged sword. It all depends on how we use it.

If we use knowledge with humility, courage, and an open mind, then it will become the best ally in our success. On the contrary, if we use knowledge with arrogance, fear, and intransigence, then it will become the source of our stagnation and failure.

10

Joy Is Different from Pleasure

Joyful souls experience pleasure without losing themselves in it. Joyless souls, however, become addicted to pleasure in ways that only engender suffering.

As we go about life experiencing all it has to offer, let us make sure we differentiate between joy and pleasure. Joy is what we experience in every life situation when we are at peace with ourselves. It is the result of realizing the divinity of our own existence, the gift of every breath, and the blessing of being able to pursue self-realization. Joy comes from within. It is the true gift of wisdom. If necessary, joy will coexist with pain to keep us strong and hopeful.

Pleasure, on the other hand, comes from the outside. It is a sensory experience that is agreeable for the body, relaxing for the mind, and expansive for the soul. However, a joyless soul will easily mistake pleasure for joy. And, since pleasure is always temporary, the desire for additional pleasure can easily enslave an empty soul.

As can be seen, there is nothing wrong with pleasure per se. Yet, for a joyless soul, pleasure can be the path to self-destruction.

Too much food causes indigestion. Too much alcohol causes inebriation. Too much of anything causes saturation and sickness. If we know when to stop, all pleasures remain as such. However, if we let ourselves be carried away without restraint, all pleasures lead to suffering and death.

Being able to build a life based on joy rather than pleasure is key to a successful life. People who find joy in everything they do, regardless of whether or not they achieve a specific goal, are more likely to learn from both victory and defeat. By the same token, they are also more likely to succeed in the end.

On the other hand, people driven mainly by the pursuit of pleasure tend to lose focus very easily, as they get high on victory but extremely down on defeat. This makes their pursuit of success highly erratic and likely to fail. In order to compensate for such a bumpy emotional ride, they tend to develop the kind of addictions, obsessions, and compulsions that sabotage everything they work for.

11

Balance Is Meant to Be Temporary

Definitive balance equals death. Life is the relentless pursuit of finite periods of balance.

Definitive balance equals stagnation and death. Even the very fundamentals of biology dictate that there must always be some degree of imbalance for life to happen. For example, in order for a cell to be alive, it must exchange fluids (e.g. nutrients and waste) with its surroundings. This means the cell must be unbalanced and in pursuit of balance. If the cell stopped interacting with its environment for no longer needing to absorb nutrients nor expel waste, then the cell would be perfectly balanced, that is, dead.

So, as we seek balance in any aspect of our lives (i.e. family, business, politics, etc.), we must also welcome unexpected imbalances. This is how the unknown reveals itself, learning becomes possible, and evolution happens.

For example, the best way to stimulate businesses to innovate and create new economic value is by welcoming the market imbalances brought about by new competitors. Without new competition, the potential new economic value may never be realized.

Nonetheless, biology also tells us that, for life to continue, all imbalances must occur within certain parameters. If a living cell becomes unbalanced past a certain point, it will also die. For example, most cell groups can tolerate fluctuations in pH or oxygen levels only within a certain range. Fluctuations outside that range kill the cells. As it turns out, life has a tolerance regarding the alterations it is able to metabolize. This is also so in every realm of human existence.

For example, the free-market economy thrives as long as every economic actor is allowed to take risks by introducing new products and services that may be of value to consumers. However, when an economic actor gains so much power as to lobby legislation that makes it difficult for new economic actors to enter the marketplace, or for consumers to switch suppliers, then the free-market economy starts to die. In short, capitalism flourishes in the imbalance created by competition, but starts to die in the imbalance created by a rigged system.

Therefore, as we develop the necessary flexibility and resilience to handle the imbalances that will inevitably occur as we pursue success, we must still preserve the basic conditions required for our pursuit to remain possible. In other words, we must make sure imbalances do not compromise the basic principles that support modern society. Such principles include democracy, the universal declaration of human rights, the free-market economy, and many other key social and economic principles that allow for the highest expression of the human condition.

12

Conflict Resolution Is a Necessity

Since balance is meant to be temporary, conflict resolution is a necessity.

As we strive for balance in our lives, we tend to focus on those concerns that are currently causing the most stress. We do this either purposefully or accidentally. For example, if we are struggling financially and, therefore, want to achieve financial stability, we will tend to seek profitable sources of income so we can cover our present and future economic needs.

However, since all aspects of life are intrinsically interconnected (i.e. family, business, community, nation, etc.), the balance we seek in a specific area will likely affect another in unintended ways, maybe disturbing our own overall balance or the balance someone else is seeking. For example, as we seek financial stability, we might focus most of our time and energy on work while unintentionally neglecting our family and friends. Consequently, conflict will inevitably arise, sooner or later, either within our own family or social circle.

Conflicts are a reminder that people are different and pursue different objectives. As long as people's objectives are not mutually exclusive regarding each other's right to freedom and the pursuit of happiness, all resulting conflicts can, in theory, be resolved. It requires hard work, an open mind, the suspension of prejudice, and skillful negotiation. And, when done right, it makes communities, businesses, and nations stronger.

In fact, success can come our way in unexpected forms as a result of resolving a conflict with another party. Different points of view about the same subject are usually the seed of a conflict. But when resolved, such differences may reveal a hidden synergy potential that benefits all partied involved. Therefore, conflict resolution is at the heart of many great steps forward in personal relationships, business practices, public policy, scientific innovations, and every other realm of human life.

13

A Vision for the Future Must Contain a Worldview

A vision for the future must reframe the past. Otherwise, it is condemned to repeat it.

Success starts with a vision for the future. However, imagining the future without reframing the past is a futile exercise. The past has a specific weight that defines the present and, if unchanged, will also outline the future.[5]

Our history shapes our current worldview because it is the source of our deepest beliefs about how the world works. And since our beliefs describe what we consider possible, they also limit what we are able to imagine for the times ahead. Therefore, if we want a future that is truly different from our history, we must reinterpret our most significant prior experiences. This way, we can examine our most deeply-held beliefs and transform those that no longer assist us in building the life we want. In so doing, we reassess ourselves, rebuild our worldview, and redefine our vision. In fact, the principles presented in this book are intended to help us do just that.

14

People Are the Mirrors of Truth

Every thought we have and every emotion we feel is connected to someone else. This is always so either directly or indirectly. That is why the only way to know our inner self is through our relationships.

Trying to master our inner self by being alone is like trying to become a good swimmer without ever going into the water. Even if we practice every swim style on dry land every day, we will still not experience the imperative need to hold our breath. Similarly, even if we explore every corner of our soul while being alone, we will still not experience how an insult or a compliment can affect our heartbeat.

Being truly at peace with oneself requires that one maintain said peace in public. So-called inner peace which is easily disturbed when in public is just unaddressed inner turmoil temporally appeased by solitude.

Whether we feel calm or restless, happy or sad, enlightened or confused, our interactions with other people will evoke our inner truth. Maybe we can hide it from them, but we can never hide it from ourselves. It is by acknowledging and embracing our inner truth, as it is revealed to us through our interactions with others, that we finally start to master ourselves.[6]

Success is, partly, a function of how much we let our relationships show us our inner truth. This helps us realize what we need to do to become the person we want to be. People who refuse to see their true self in their relationships with others may seem successful on the surface, but they will always feel uncomfortable with the world around them. It is impossible to enjoy success completely while experiencing such aggravation. Only when we let others help us discover ourselves on a daily basis is it possible to experience success fully.

15

Hope Can Become the Best Cover-up for Fear

As we hope for the best, we must work for the best.

We all have heard the expressions, "Never give up hope" and "Hope dies last." These are powerful statements that can make an important difference in times of struggle.

Hope is a major piece of the human psyche. It gives us the necessary confidence to keep a positive attitude in the midst of hardship. In this way, we reduce our levels of anxiety, avoid despair, and summon the necessary strength to keep fighting for what we want, despite unimaginable difficulties.

However, if hope is not properly nourished and effectively used, it can turn into numb waiting. In other words, hope can become a disguise for surrender and fear. In order to be truly effective in the pursuit of our goals, hope must be coupled with determination, courage, and action. Otherwise, fear and conformism will sneak in, making inaction the only result of hope.

Successful people have a strong sense of hope. Most importantly, though, they use hope as fuel for action; not as a sedative to justify inaction.

16

Perseverance Is the Key to Patience

Patience without perseverance is just surrender.

Achieving a worthy objective takes time. Time is an intrinsic part of success. In such a process, disappointment will most likely come our way before any sign of success appears on the horizon. Waiting is inevitable.

As the wait becomes longer, our commitment and enthusiasm are tested—we start to wonder whether our pursuit is worthwhile. We start to wonder whether we are capable of achieving the sought objective. This is when we have to choose between giving up and keeping up. This is when we are really faced with the choice between resignation and patience.

Resignation will cause us to abandon our quest and deny our very selves. Patience, on the contrary, will allow us to rediscover ourselves over and over until success is inevitable. This is why patience and perseverance are absolutely synonymous. That who waits and does not persevere has surrendered.

17

Self-knowledge Must Be Actionable

As we pursue self-knowledge, let us make sure we do not lose ourselves in the depths of reflection.

Exploring our inner self and developing self-knowledge is very much like crawling into a deep dark hole full of unknowns in pursuit of a worthy jewel.

Let us imagine a hypothetical excursion, in which we want to see what is inside of a deep dark hole. To do so successfully, we must crawl into it as deeply as we can. Yet the deeper we go, the dimmer the light, making the exploration scarier and more dangerous. An appropriate source of light is crucial for the expedition to be successful. If we cannot see, then the excursion is useless. So, how do we illuminate our path down the hole?

We can bring a flashlight with us, but, eventually, the batteries will run out and we will have to go back out to the surface to replace them. We can also bring a wired source of light, but the wire has a limited length and is connected to some source of power located also on the surface. Therefore, there is no exploring the depths of a hole without keeping a connection to the outside. If we lose sight of the latter, we will lose ourselves in the former. Only by knowing where the surface is can we go into the hole and come back to tell others what we saw.

The process of self-discovery is very similar to the hypothetical excursion. As we explore our inner self in pursuit of self-knowledge, we had better do it with a solid foot in our everyday reality. We must dig into our unconscious with a clear, pragmatic purpose. We must have clarity as to what aspects of our daily lives we want to change. Success is directly proportional to our ability to explore the deepest corners of our soul and, later, apply our findings in ways that are practical, valuable, and enjoyable in the outside world.

18

Empathy Is About Self-Confidence

If we know who we are and what we want, we will be able to relate to others more effectively regardless of personal affinities.

Social dynamics are very complex. People interact in multiple ways engendering affinities and differences. This shapes our relationships at every level, including family, community, and country. Luckily, we can expand and strengthen our social networks by going beyond the initial affinities and differences we may have with others.

Sympathy, antipathy, and empathy are the three main responses we can have toward other people. Sympathy is what occurs when we approve of what another person is thinking, feeling, or doing, which usually translates into feelings of allegiance and actions of support. Antipathy, on the other hand, is what happens when we disapprove of what another individual is thinking, feeling, or doing, which usually translates into criticism and separation. Interestingly, empathy gives us the ability to choose our best response to another person's thoughts, feelings, and actions, regardless of whether we initially felt sympathy or antipathy toward them, in order to pursue a higher purpose of collective impact.

It is paramount to point out that true empathy is not about being artificial, putting on a poker face, and manipulating others. Empathy is about having enough self-confidence as to be able to validate and support another individual's motivations, as different as they may be from our own, as long as they do not collide with our ethical code. In fact, in cases of extreme personal growth, empathy can lead us to modify our ethical code as a result of acknowledging the legitimate rights of another person with whom we initially had little in common.

By doing this, we help others find the best within themselves as we find the best within ourselves. Thus, by being empathetic, we can achieve synergies that would otherwise be impossible. Empathy is, in fact, one of the most valuable interpersonal skills and, in this regard, a key to success.

19

Guilt Alone Engenders No Virtue

Whoever feels responsible seeks a solution. Whoever feels only guilty, though, feels unworthy and expects to be punished, which clouds the judgment necessary to find a solution.

Guilt alone makes us feel tense, fearful, and unworthy. Interestingly, from that emotional space, it can lead us to either irresponsibility or responsibility, depending on how we handle it.

When guilt takes us down the path of irresponsibility, it does so in one of two ways. On the one hand, it can drive us to self-flagellation motivated by deep feelings of shame and unworthiness. On the other hand, it can prompt us to blatantly blame innocent people in order to avoid public embarrassment and potential punishment. In neither case would we be owning up to our actions nor experiencing any learning. That is, we would be behaving irresponsibly.

However, guilt can also take us down the path of responsibility if we decide to transcend the shame and fear that come with the former. In this case, we would no longer feel the need to either self-flagellate or project our guilt onto others. We would be in a position to face the consequences of our actions publicly. Should such consequences be negative, responsibility would allow us to apologize, compensate those affected, and learn from our mistakes. Likewise, it would encourage us to share our learnings with others so that they, too, can benefit.

Success is directly proportional to our level of responsibility and inversely proportional to our level of guilt. When we are at fault, we must work internally to hold ourselves accountable instead of just feeling guilty. Responsibility is expansive, while guilt is restrictive. Responsibility allows us to learn from both our mistakes and our achievements so that we can keep improving until success is inevitable. On the contrary, guilt will cloud our judgment, thus making learning almost impossible. Whether it leads us down the path of self-flagellation or outright avoidance, guilt will make success an unlikely outcome.

20

Democracy Is a Daily Conquest

Tyranny must be defeated every day.

Every democracy has been preceded by some form of totalitarian government, be it a monarchy, a dictatorship, or foreign colonialism. Therefore, democracy has always been the result of a struggle, a battle, or a war. Once conquered, democracy prevails only as long as its citizens become actively involved in its never-ending preservation.

Inevitably, the forces of tyranny always lurk in the dark corners of every democratic society and will attack it by its weakest point—extreme economic inequality. Democracy becomes exceptionally weak when, despite its promise to secure people's right to life, liberty, and the pursuit of happiness, poverty becomes widespread, a good education becomes unattainable for most, and wealth becomes concentrated in very few hands. Tyrants know this and use it in their favor.

While tyrants of times past used to reach power by the use of arms, modern ones often reach power by electoral vote. Their most valuable resource is the hopelessness of the least privileged and the most discontent; their promise is some form of social vindication; and their strategy is deceit.

Once tyrants reach power, however, their initial promise devolves into vengeance against all who express the slightest form of dissent. Furthermore, they institutionalize fear in order to sever all remaining traces of hope. Finally, once they have taken democracy hostage, tyrants make sure it becomes practically impossible to regain it by votes alone. A struggle, a battle, or even a war will again be necessary to reclaim democracy.

Democracy is the art and science of living in freedom while respecting the freedom of others. Put differently, democracy is the only form of government that promotes order while respecting individual liberties. Hence, only in democracy is success a credible aspiration for everyone. In tyranny, on the contrary, all possibilities of success basically disappear for anyone who does not submit to the regime's authority. Therefore, if we want to pursue success in freedom, we must do everything within our reach to keep democracy alive and eradicate extreme economic inequality, democracy's worst enemy.

21

Nations Rely on Principles to Endure

Governments, businesses, and consumers must not let the law of supply and demand supersede democratic principles. When they do, the result is always some form of tyranny.

Throughout history, the nations of the world have repeatedly, and often painfully, learned the following four lessons:

1. When governments and businesses become unconditional allies, consumers are abused and a recession is inevitable. By the same token, when governments and consumers become unconditional allies, businesses are abused and a recession is inevitable. The former is the path of the extreme right; the latter is the path of the extreme left. It is time for the peoples of the world not to let themselves be seduced by either.

2. By design, in a healthy economy, individuals and businesses leverage their operations by using banks as financial intermediaries. When this order is reversed, that is, when banks use individuals and businesses as financial intermediaries through

questionable forms of lending and debt collection, the result is always an economic catastrophe.

3. The worst enemy of democracy and free market is widespread poverty, which, in turn, is the ideal breeding ground for all forms of tyranny. In this regard, all democratic governments must do everything in their power to help in the economic recovery of those who have fallen behind as a result of the imperfections of the free-market economy. They must do so through education and the stimulation of investments focused on employment generation and economic growth.

4. Democracy is the art and science of living in freedom while respecting the freedom of others. This statement makes conflict inevitable and conflict resolution a necessity. Therefore, the highest forms of justice and peace available to the peoples of the world depend on the levels of individual and social consciousness they are able to attain.

The nations that value these lessons and implement policies based on them see their people prosper and succeed. On the contrary, nations that ignore these lessons see their people suffer in unimaginable ways.

References

[1] Harper, D. (2012). Online Etymology Dictionary. Retrieved from http://www.etymonline.com/index.php?term=opportunity&allowed_in_frame=0

[2] Romero, Luis E. (2013). Blog post *"You Are the Opportunity You Were Waiting For."* Retrieved from http://leromero.com/blog/2013/7/30/opportunity

[3] Romero, Luis E. (2012). *The Seventh Distinction: The Path to Personal Mastery, Leadership & Peak Performance*. Miami, FL: Luis Romero International, Page 87.

[4] Ibid., Page 82.

[5] Ibid., Page 65.

[6] Ibid., Page 83.

www.ingramcontent.com/pod-product-compliance
Lightning Source LLC
LaVergne TN
LVHW041209080426
835508LV00008B/869